A Di... Mural

Sally Cowan

Photographs by Lindsay Edwards

Contents

Goal	2
Materials	2
Steps	4
Glossary	16

Goal

To make a dinosaur mural

Materials

You will need:
- a big sheet of paper
- green and blue paint
- yellow, brown, and green cardboard
- scissors
- glue
- a marker

3

Steps

1. Paint the paper blue for the sky and green for the forest floor.

   Let the paint dry.

5

2. Cut the yellow cardboard into **shapes**:

- one half of a circle for the **body**
- one rectangle for the head
- four smaller rectangles for the legs
- one long triangle for the tail

Then cut:
- ten small triangles for the **spikes**

3. Glue the body onto the mural.

4. Glue the head, the legs, and the tail onto the body to make the dinosaur.

9

5. Glue the ten small triangles along the dinosaur's back.

6. Draw an eye and a mouth on the dinosaur's head.

7. Cut long strips of green cardboard to make some leaves.

8. Glue the strips onto the mural to make the plants.

9. Cut round shapes from the brown cardboard to make some rocks.

10. Glue them onto the mural.

11. Put the mural on the wall.

Glossary

body

shapes

spikes